DISCARD

Influential Presidents
Theodore Roosevelt

by Emma Huddleston

www.focusreaders.com

Copyright © 2023 by Focus Readers®, Lake Elmo, MN 55042. All rights reserved. No part of this book may be reproduced or utilized in any form or by any means without written permission from the publisher.

Focus Readers is distributed by North Star Editions:
sales@northstareditions.com | 888-417-0195

Produced for Focus Readers by Red Line Editorial.

Photographs ©: Library of Congress, cover, 1, 19; Ann Ronan Picture Library/Heritage Images/Newscom, 4; Shutterstock Images, 7, 11, 13, 20–21, 25, 27; AP Images, 8, 14, 22, 29; Historica Graphica Collection/Heritage Images/Newscom, 17

Library of Congress Cataloging-in-Publication Data
Names: Huddleston, Emma, author.
Title: Theodore Roosevelt / Emma Huddleston.
Description: Lake Elmo, MN : Focus Readers, [2023] | Series: [Influential presidents] | Includes index. | Audience: Grades 2-3
Identifiers: LCCN 2022030297 (print) | LCCN 2022030298 (ebook) | ISBN 9781637394670 (hardcover) | ISBN 9781637395042 (paperback) | ISBN 9781637395752 (pdf) | ISBN 9781637395417 (ebook)
Subjects: LCSH: Roosevelt, Theodore, 1858-1919--Juvenile literature. | Presidents--United States--Biography--Juvenile literature.
Classification: LCC E757 .H89 2023 (print) | LCC E757 (ebook) | DDC 973.91/1092 [B]--dc23/eng/20220623
LC record available at https://lccn.loc.gov/2022030297
LC ebook record available at https://lccn.loc.gov/2022030298

Printed in the United States of America
Mankato, MN
012023

About the Author

Emma Huddleston lives in Minnesota with her husband and daughter. She enjoys reading, writing, and staying active. She thinks learning about presidents is an important part of understanding how the United States works today.

Table of Contents

CHAPTER 1
Death of a President 5

CHAPTER 2
From Soldier to Governor 9

CHAPTER 3
The Reformer 15

ISSUE SPOTLIGHT
Parks and Forests 20

CHAPTER 4
The Square Deal 23

Focus on Theodore Roosevelt • 28
Glossary • 30
To Learn More • 31
Index • 32

Chapter 1

Death of a President

In September 1901, Vice President Theodore Roosevelt was about to give a speech in Vermont. But he got some terrible news. President William McKinley had been shot.

The man who shot President McKinley hid his gun under a piece of cloth.

Roosevelt left right away. He went to New York to see the president.

McKinley had **surgery**. Doctors thought he would recover. So, a few days later, Roosevelt went on vacation. But then he got a message. McKinley's health was getting worse. Roosevelt left to see

Did You Know?

Roosevelt was the youngest person to become president.

 Theodore Roosevelt becomes president after the death of William McKinley.

him again. However, McKinley died before Roosevelt arrived.

As a result, Roosevelt became the new president. He was only 42 years old. Even so, he was eager to lead the United States.

Chapter 2

From Soldier to Governor

Theodore Roosevelt was born on October 27, 1858. He grew up in New York. As a child, Theodore was often sick. He could not go to school. So, tutors taught him at home.

 As a college student, Roosevelt was known for his high energy.

Theodore got healthier as he grew up. Eventually, he went to Harvard College. He then went to Columbia Law School for a few years. But he left school to do other jobs. He was interested in writing and **politics**.

In 1881, Roosevelt ran for office. He was only 23 years old. He became the youngest member of the New York State Assembly. There he became known as a reformer. That means he tried to change the way government worked. Most

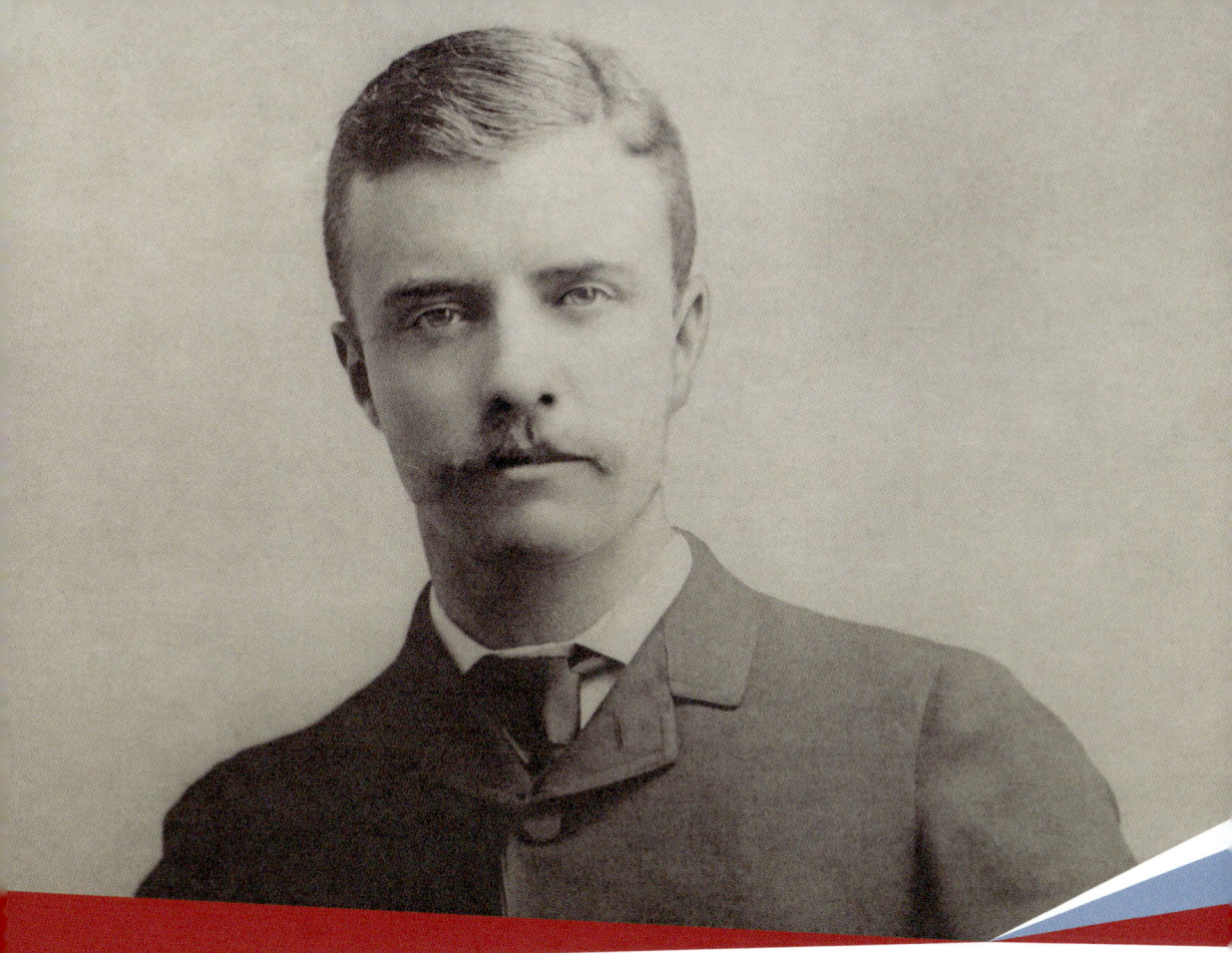

▶ **Roosevelt served in the New York State Assembly for three years.**

of all, Roosevelt wanted to stop **corruption**. He had several ideas for how to do that. But only a few of his ideas became law.

In 1897, Roosevelt became a military leader. He was in charge of a group of soldiers. They fought in the Spanish-American War (1898). The United States won the war. Roosevelt was a national hero.

Roosevelt was elected governor of New York in 1898. As governor,

Did You Know?

After the Spanish-American War, the United States took over several islands from Spain.

 In the military, Roosevelt's group was known as the Rough Riders.

he made several changes. He signed laws to help workers. He also created programs to protect the **environment**.

Chapter 3

The Reformer

President McKinley was running for reelection in 1900. He picked Theodore Roosevelt as his vice president. The pair promised to make fair laws for workers and help businesses earn more money.

 Roosevelt gives a fiery speech during the 1900 election.

15

McKinley and Roosevelt won the election. But in 1901, McKinley was killed. Roosevelt became president.

In 1902, Roosevelt dealt with a major **strike**. Coal miners wanted better pay. And they didn't want to work as many hours. Mine owners would not agree to the workers'

Did You Know?

Before the 1900 election, Roosevelt traveled and gave speeches. He stopped in more than 450 cities.

 People line up for coal to heat their homes during the 1902 coal strike.

demands. The strike lasted months. The country was low on coal.

Roosevelt helped the two sides reach a deal. Mine owners gave the workers slightly higher pay. They also made the workday shorter.

17

In return, workers agreed to go back to their jobs.

Roosevelt also worked to limit big companies. For example, several railroad companies had joined together. They created one huge company. It controlled most railroads in the West. Roosevelt thought it had too much power. He broke up the company. This action made him popular with voters.

In the early 1900s, nearly all voters were white men. Most

 In the early 1900s, railroads were an important form of transportation.

women and most Black people were not allowed to vote. As president, Roosevelt did not try to help them gain this right.

ISSUE SPOTLIGHT

Parks and Forests

In 1883, Theodore Roosevelt took a trip to North Dakota. He hunted and explored the land. The trip changed his life. Roosevelt became interested in wildlife. Later, he made laws to protect the environment.

As president, Roosevelt was known for park and forestry programs. He set aside more land for national parks than all presidents before him. He also created many protected areas for birds. Roosevelt wanted to make sure people could always enjoy these parts of the country.

Roosevelt created five new national parks, including Crater Lake in Oregon.

Chapter 4

The Square Deal

Theodore Roosevelt ran for a second **term** in 1904. He promised voters a "Square Deal." He would support laws to help both workers and companies. Many voters liked this plan.

Roosevelt waves to a crowd during the 1904 election.

23

Roosevelt won the 1904 election easily. He signed several laws in his second term. One law made food safer. Some companies had been using dangerous ingredients. The new law held them responsible for the safety of their food.

Roosevelt also helped with shipping. In the early 1900s, sending goods from coast to coast was difficult. Ships had to go all the way around South America. US leaders wanted a faster route.

 Roosevelt speaks to workers as they build the Panama Canal in 1906.

So, Roosevelt made a deal with Panama. The United States would build a **canal** there. It would connect the Atlantic and Pacific Oceans. That way, ships could travel a much shorter distance.

Roosevelt's second term ended in 1909. Three years later, he ran for president again. This time, he planned to improve **welfare**. He also wanted to make new trade laws. And he wanted to give women the right to vote. However, he lost the election.

The Panama Canal opened in 1914. The United States controlled it for many years. But in 1999, Panama gained control.

 Roosevelt delivers a speech during his unsuccessful 1912 run for president.

Roosevelt died on January 6, 1919. Many people remembered him for the Square Deal. They also remembered his work to protect the environment.

FOCUS ON
Theodore Roosevelt

Write your answers on a separate piece of paper.

1. In your own words, explain the Square Deal.
2. Do you think national parks are important? Why or why not?
3. When did Roosevelt fight in a war?
   - **A.** 1858
   - **B.** 1898
   - **C.** 1901
4. How did the Panama Canal help the United States?
   - **A.** It made shipping easier because routes were much shorter.
   - **B.** It helped end the war between the United States and Spain.
   - **C.** It stopped travel between the Atlantic and Pacific Oceans.

5. What does **tutors** mean in this book?

*As a child, Theodore was often sick. He could not go to school. So, **tutors** taught him at home.*

    A. schools where sick children get healthier
    B. illnesses that make it difficult to learn
    C. people who teach students outside of school

6. What does **route** mean in this book?

*Ships had to go all the way around South America. US leaders wanted a faster **route**.*

    A. a leader of a country
    B. a path to travel
    C. a fast ship

Answer key on page 32.

Glossary

canal
A long, human-made ditch that allows water to flow from one area to another.

corruption
Dishonest or illegal acts, especially by powerful people.

environment
The natural surroundings of living things in a particular place.

politics
Activities that have to do with laws and government.

strike
When people stop working as a way to demand better working conditions or better pay.

surgery
A medical procedure to fix a problem inside the body.

term
The amount of time a person can serve after being elected.

welfare
Help given to people in need.

To Learn More

BOOKS

Doudna, Kelly. *Building the Panama Canal.* Minneapolis: Abdo Publishing, 2018.

Gaines, Ann Graham. *Theodore Roosevelt.* Mankato, MN: The Child's World, 2020.

Reynolds, A. M. *Theodore Roosevelt.* North Mankato, MN: Capstone Press, 2021.

NOTE TO EDUCATORS

Visit **www.focusreaders.com** to find lesson plans, activities, links, and other resources related to this title.

Index

C
college, 10
corruption, 11

E
environment, 13, 20, 27

G
governor, 12

M
McKinley, William, 5–7, 15–16

N
national parks, 20
New York State Assembly, 10

P
Panama Canal, 25–26

R
railroads, 18

S
Spanish-American War, 12
Square Deal, 23, 27
strike, 16–17

V
vice president, 5, 15
voting rights, 18–19, 26

W
welfare, 26
workers, 13, 15–18, 23

Answer Key: 1. Answers will vary; 2. Answers will vary; 3. B; 4. A; 5. C; 6. B